CW01512276

What rhymes with Mum?

Leander Partington

Mum Chat

You said it was traumatic,
He tore you, front to back.
Now every time you try to poo
you fear your vag will crack.

Those sutures are still painful,
and sitting is a joke.
You felt six thousand stitches
when you had a little poke.

You cry for your vagina;
it will never be the same...
Hang on, I'm sorry, how rude of me!
I haven't asked your name.

Don't Forget the Mum

The baby's arrived,
it's so crowded inside.
There's cooing and aahhing galore.
But nobody sees
the new mum on her knees.
She's the one they haplessly ignore.

The Dad's been misled,
he's wetting the head,
when the Mum really needs him at home.
But in all the excitement
they forget who's important;
She's starting to feel all alone.

A general rule of thumb,
when visiting a new mum,
whether it's her first, second or fifth:
Don't ignore her achievement
of creating this infant,
So make sure you bring HER a gift.

Well, We Tried.

I'd had a glass of wine,
- I lie, it was more like three –
and in my sexiest voice, I said,
"Come upstairs with me".

But when we reached the bedroom,
mum guilt took hold of me.
"We can't have sex with him in there"
- but hubby did not agree.

"He won't know what's going on.
I doubt he'll even stir.
We can make sure we're really quiet,
and stay covered if you prefer."

"I won't be able to concentrate.
I'll stop then not resume.
Let's try again in four months' time,
when he's moved to his own room."

Still Me

Congratulations, you've had a baby!
(The metaphorical switch is flicked)
All the moments that made you, you,
will be totally eclipsed.

Conversational content's now constrained,
regardless of your history.
And just like that, motherhood
erases your identity.

You might have travelled round the world,
Or been a CEO.
You might be fixing up a car,
But, all this will never show.

For once you share your exciting news,
"We're pregnant" you'll exclaim
You'll likely lose your entire past
including your first name.

This disregard for who we were
appears accepted by society.
Chat to the person, not just the mum:
We're still us, still you, still me.

Today You Broke My Heart

Your laughter is infectious and your smile
Can melt a thousand hearts with just one glance.
All those late nights and pacing for a mile,
Just one loving look has me in a trance.

All manner of problems will drift away
As you stare up at me with that wide grin.
The happy tears are a small price to pay
Feeling them tumble down towards my chin.

This one moment is so overwhelming
You're warm, you're happy, you're full, you're secure,
The love you emit is unrelenting,
Straight from your heart, a love that is pure.

Sorry it took a while to feel this way.
From now on I will love you more each day.

Birthday Parties

What happened to bumps
and musical chairs?
Pass the parcel and
kids everywhere?

It seems like the world
has increased expectations
when planning your child's
big birthday celebrations.

Now, a first birthday party's
not complete unless
there's a glass of champagne
and a posh evening dress.

Then you must up your game
when your baby turns two
and supervise twelve toddlers
at the local petting zoo.

Now three is quite tricky
because they'll all need the loo

so booking a play centre
may be perfect for you.

At four years old
they're starting to remember
so you'll have to outdo
Jack's party last November.

He had a magician
a DJ and a clown,
and hired a hall
for a blow-up playground.

Five, Six and Seven
you need to think big
a mocktail spa party
or a REAL Dinosaur dig.

Now at nine years old
You'll need to re-mortgage
to fund a trip pony trekking
or an overseas voyage.

By the time that they're 10
they'll want independence,
so plan an Ibiza party
without adults in attendance.

For an 11-year-old
just speak to the Queen
and hire Buckingham Palace
for an afternoon tea.

Luckily by 12 extravagance
they'll be near the teen stage
so book a ticket for Mars
then stand back and wave.

Well, I'm Not.

"How are you feeling, love?", they say.
But, I don't know how to reply.
There's a liquid fear sliding down my throat
and I'm being suffocated inside.

"How are you coping, love?", they ask.
When I know I'm obviously not.
Why's there an assumption that I must cope?
I'm learning to deal with an awful lot.

I haven't had a full night's sleep,
My mind has turned to mush.
I feel I'm always on high alert.
This mum thing's really tough.

"How can I help you, love?", they say.
Just pop over for a friendly chat.
Let me feel like I'm not alone in this,
It's overwhelming from where I'm sat.

"What do you need, love?", they ask.
Take the reins for just a morning.
Let me not cope til I've figured it out,
without making me feel like I'm not coping.

Blocked

Movicol: Isn't it prescribed
when you're blocked up inside
and the shit that you feel, can't escape?
That uncomfortable feeling,
just downright depressing.
Dark matter of an awkward shape.

Knowing it needs to come out but scared that it will
hurt.
Knowing that you will feel better immediately
afterwards.
Knowing that ignoring it will not make it disappear.
Knowing that it is visible on the outside.

But no prescription of laxatives
can remove this blockage from my body.
This heavy, weighty shadow that consumes me,
Steals my smile, removes my happiness, extracts my
desires.
They ask:
"How are you in yourself?"
I'm blocked.

Mum Truths

There are things they don't tell you
when you first become a Mum
like the sinking realisation
of what you've become.

They don't warn you about
hormonal sweating at night,
the alarming hair loss,
a constant internal fight.

They don't prepare you mentally
for the thoughts you might get:
the negative intrusions,
a slight hint of regret.

They don't make you aware
you can feel severely alone,
even when you're with the baby,
for reasons unknown.

They don't always inform us:
it doesn't always come naturally,
we don't all get 'that bond',
Or fall in love instantaneously.

Despite these truths being concealed,
it has made us stronger than most.
Us network of mums support each other,
Our commonality? Tea and toast.

No Shame

I will dance the Oogie Boogie
with a frog hat on my head,
and blow the loudest raspberries
until my face has gone bright red.

I will race around the playground
playing dinosaurs – ROAR!
And pretend I'm being chased by sharks
by swimming on the floor.

I'll knee slide to celebrate,
we will laugh, sing and shout.
Don't judge me, just join me
- it's what parenting's all about!

One for the Dads

Keep an eye on your man
as mental health can
target the strongest of blokes.

Being a Dad can be tough
(we know parenting's rough).
It's different for all kinds of folks.

There's lots of support
for mums so distraught,
but some dads are too scared to say.

So, if your dad-friend feels blue,
just start with a brew,
and a chat asking, "Are you ok?"

She Wakes at Two.

It wasn't a question,
but a response to conversation.
Just a statement, to be precise.
Yet they pour out their advice:

Have you tried reducing her nap?
Have you tried a white noise app?
Have you tried letting her cry?
Have you tried googling why?
Have you tried researching her leap?
Have you tried driving her to sleep?
Have you tried wrapping her tight?
Have you tried a little night light?

She's only four months old,
she still needs my hand to hold.
If she still needs me in the night,
for me, that is perfectly alright.

I Wore Them

He would tell me a story,
or whisper in my ear,
Or sing me a song
Of what he could see and hear.

She would be so cosy
on the front, safe and dry.
I could hear each tiny snuffle
and act on every cry.

In the sling or in the backpack,
I wore them close to me.
Not only for their benefit
but the sense of being free.

No queuing for the lifts,
No negotiating a pram round shops,
They were safely strapped to me;
(*and with nowhere else to go*)
it prevented toddler strops.

Is She Good?

Poop shoots from the top of her nappy.
Three times a night, she steals sleep.
She carefully aims her projectile vomit.
She postpones her three month 'leap'.

She regularly exercises her lungs.
Hot meals and coffee are disturbed.
Daily conversations are interrupted.
Her irregular breath leaves me perturbed.

Is this what constitutes as being 'Good'?
Does this conform to your expectation?
She is doing exactly what a baby should do.
In my eyes, she is perfection.

I Needed Someone

I needed someone to hate,
so I hated you.

I needed someone to blame,
so I blamed you.

I needed someone to doubt,
so I doubted you.

I needed someone to control,
so I controlled you.

I needed someone to ignore,
so I ignored you.

I needed someone to forget,
so I forgot you.

Four-in-a-Bed

Why do we have
a three bedroom house
When we end up asleep in one bed?

They have a room each
but want to co-sleep:
Two parents, two children and Ted.

Their feet start to scurry,
They come in with a hurry
complaining of nightmares or thirst.

 We should just get a tent
and save on the rent
but safety and comfort come first.

The Good Ones

A full participant of the 'night duty' team.
Administering medicines and magic cream.
Creating stories with awesome voices,
ensuring all characters have equal choices.

Negotiating terms with dinner-time veg.
Protecting them from bears hiding in the hedge.
Instilling a sense of right and wrong.
Helping them understand where they belong.

Playing the hundredth game of peek-a-boo.
Unperturbed when dealing with poo.
Supporting my hobbies and work-life display.
Opening the wine at the end of the day.

Demonstrating love and solidarity.
Sharing the parenting responsibility.

Cracked

And then I cracked
Like furrows of dried plaster.
Before, immaculately seamless,
Now a silhouette of mountains,
foreboding; fearful apprehension.

It doesn't weaken me.
My structural integrity is still unbroken,
but I see it every day.
I know it is there.
I anticipate its expansion.

But, this time others can see it.
Comforted to know that they can recognise it.
We're maintaining vigilance.

Speed Pooing

A man saunters into a toilet.
A paper, a phone, a magazine all trail in behind him.
He sits and ponders the world whilst getting on with it.
Careful consideration of the particulars.

10 minutes pass.

A mother bursts into the toilet.
The menacing monster is three shuffles away,
its beady eyes observing the open door
as the sick-stained denim passes her knees.
The same force as six months ago.
Push.
Push.
PUSH!
The familiar relief.

12 seconds have passed.
The monster, with the beady blue eyes, is at her feet.

Siblings

Don't try to wake the baby,
She's just drifted off to sleep.
Don't touch her head,
or poke her cheek,
Don't press that bloody sheep!

You will survive if you do not
cuddle, hold or kiss her.
Right now she's happy catching flies,
take a step away from your sister.

All the Feels

On **Monday**, I cried tears for no reason.

On **Tuesday**, I laughed until my cheeks burned.

On **Wednesday**, my heart ached with love.

On **Thursday**, my frustration with unwanted advice sent me over the edge.

On **Friday**, my anxiety overwhelmed me.

On **Saturday**, I hid, afraid to emerge.

On **Sunday**, I felt a cocktail of all these emotions.

Alone in ASDA

There's an emptiness which is normally occupied,
A void that exists by my left-hand side.
A space where he habitually sits,
arguing the finer points of our weekly shopping list.

But with no well-timed temper tantrums to evade
and unable to sing aloud, explain or persuade,
 I mutter my shopping list to no-one;
This unaccompanied experience is no fun.

A lonesome penguin extracted from the family huddle.
Free from distraction, yet even more in a muddle.

Chaos has stayed at home.
I'm in ASDA on my own.

Smile

I don't know how you do it,
it's a magic you possess
a contagious sparkle you emit
when we feel under duress.

Like the uncontrollable frustration
of being woken throughout the night,
which diminishes when I see your face,
somehow your smile makes it alright.

Or when I'm at the end of my tether
for you've screamed for the whole day,
and my ears are ringing from the din,
your smile magics it away.

Or the exhaustion from a day at work,
with stress levels at their highest,
a nine hour absence from each other
and I know my opinion's biased

but it feels like ice caps melting,
slowly the negativity dissolves
a grin projected through toothless gums.
I'm in awe of what love solves.

Unaware of animosity,
no malice in your innocence,
Your unconditional love thaws hate
into clouds of insignificance.

I really don't know how you do it
but it's a regular occurrence,
 rejuvenating my faith and love
just by your physical appearance.

They need to harness this magic
to spread across the world.
For no therapy or drug can match
the power your smile holds.

The Battle

It was amazing: the convenience,
But my boobs were always leaking.
She was growing so well,
But my nipples were suffering.

It was free of charge,
Except breast pads, pumps and bras.
The oxytocin high was incredible,
But some days it felt like a farce.

My boobs, they were magic,
But were exposed to the elements.
I was safe from periods,
But ached with engorgement.

I could multitask with one free hand,
But on her, I didn't concentrate.
I didn't have anything to sterilise,
But mindful of what I drank and ate.

My boobs were fabulously big,
But people stared when I fed.
We both were protected from illness,
But not from the harsh words said.

But something I didn't realise
Was the pressure from society.
We've won our breastfeeding battle and done
What felt right for her and me

Links

The direct correlation,
between hormones and lactation,
often makes itself known,
when dealing with a situation,
avoiding confrontation,
wishing we'd stayed at home.

Like cuddles with strangers,
highlighting risk assessment worthy dangers,
when I don't even know them by name.
An unknown fragrance lingers,
"What's she doing to his fingers?"
It's just hormones, I know; they're to blame.

As my planets solidify,
leaking all over my
top, bra, stomach and chest,
my temperament magnifies.
"He's only two weeks old!", I reply,
so back off, I'm doing my best.

Mugged

It has snuck up on me,
unexpectedly
robbing my sanity,
increasing my vulnerability.

I'm stepping apprehensively,
guarding incessantly,
thinking irrationally,
worrying illogically:

Mugged by anxiety.

Mum Tourette's

I swear I died; I was completely hanging,
Oh, wow, clever girl, look you're standing!
Like the last time we came down south,
Don't you put that in your mouth!
I definitely had more gin than you.
Oh dear, has someone done a poo?
We were dancing like the old Prime Minister.
Don't hit or punch your sister.
Mind you, it was a great place to meet.
Sit back on your chair nicely and eat.
How's the swelling on both your knees?
What do you say next? Please.
Knee sliding at our age is a real no go.
No. How many times do I have to say NO.
What time did we get in 2:30? 3?
Leo, do you need a wee-wee?
Let's do it again! When are you free?
Are you 100% sure you don't need a wee?

Cabbage Tits

When your milk comes in
and you're all engorged,
Who do you call?
CABBAGE TITS.

When your ducts are blocked
and your smile is forged,
Who do you call?
CABBAGE TITS.

When mastitis hits
and you need relief,
Who do you call?
CABBAGE TITS.

When you reduce supply
grab an ice-cold leaf
and you'll become
CABBAGE TITS.

Family Parking

If you park in that spot
I hope you have got
a child, or two, in your car.

Family parking ensures
our kids don't smash other doors,
thus preventing an insurance hoo-ha.

But some people are selfish,
and just plain twat-ish,
assuming these rules don't apply.

If only the authorities,
would enforce this priority
rather than turning a blind-eye.

The Map of my Bed

My bed is South America;
it's divided into territories,
with inhabitants who don't comprehend
zone-specific equalities.

My husband is Brazil
with the lion's share of the bed.
Undisturbed in comfort:
An entire pillow for his head.

My toddler, at three years old,
resembles Guyana and Peru,
with his bottom bridging in the air
reaching the edges of The Falklands too.

The baby is Argentina,
lying snuggled next to me.
Protected by maternal instinct,
cradled just above my knees.

So, I suppose that makes me Chile,
a fairly suitable name I think.
For I'm always fecking freezing
- on the edge, right on the brink.

It's Tough, But I Like It.

I complain about the pain,
and how sore it is when feeding.
I complain about being engorged
and the stains from constant leaking.

I complain about the sleepless nights,
when she feeds almost every hour.
I complain about needing breast pads,
and the let down in the shower.

But despite all this, I like it
and I really don't want to stop.
So, please, let me moan and grumble
until I decide to swap.

Co-Sleeping

I will NEVER co-sleep.
I categorically said.
I will never have my kids
sleep in my own bed.

Unless they are cold
or feeling too hot,
got a tummy that's hurting
or covered in snot.

Or if they've been frightened
by a nasty nightmare.
Or any other time when they
just need you there.

Hang on...

Just Be There

I give myself a pep talk
before I go to bed
to stifle anxious thoughts
that dance around my head.

I strive to distract my mind
with what we've done that day,
I'm warding off the monsters,
making them go away.

But then the cold consumes me
with a tingle in my head.
My body starts to panic;
an overwhelming sense of dread.

I don't yet know the triggers
Or how long I will be haunted.
But please don't think I'm crazy,
I just need to be supported.

Late Risers

This morning,
I woke up naturally.
Then panic crept in instead.
Normally by 7:30,
I have a toddler in my bed.

But there I was alone,
with an awful sense of dread.
I have never moved so quickly,
for fear that they were dead.

Alive and snoring happily,
just fast asleep instead.
My strong maternal instincts
playing havoc with my head.

This Mum Is…

… Tired. Beyond tired. A Zombie.
… Making waffles, beans and cheese for tea.

… Never sure if I'm getting it right.
… Going out with the girls tonight.

… Wondering how the bills will get paid.
… Amazed by what my body has made.

… Going to require a padded bra.
… Chatting about my episiotomy scar.

… Looking forward to returning to work.
… Fed up with my toddler acting like a jerk.

… Ridiculously excited by the new hoover.
… Longing for this day to be over.

… Currently covered in snot, sick and pee.
… Taking a moment just for me.
… Pouring a giant G&T.

Dirty Mum

I've had more costume changes than Madonna in
Evita,
and am surrounded by laundry on all of the heaters.
If you walked through my door and took a look at my
outfit,
You'd be forgiven for thinking that I had just lost it.
For I am adorned in my best dress and slippers,
and once they are sicked on, it's joggers and flippers.
It's too early in the day to put my wedding dress on,
but believe me, it'll be next once the joggers are gone.
Yes, you have guessed it, I've spent the whole day
covered in bodily fluids in some kind of way.
Be it sick or poo, or both in succession,
Will I ever be clean? Based on that facial expression...

No.

Mastitis

My apologies for writing
An acrostic about mastitis.
Shitty mastitis that hurts like hell.
Tender boobs that if anyone comes near
I will rip them a new one.
Torturous, painful lumps and bumps.
It's a shame mastitis doesn't have an F in it.
Shitty, fucking mastitis.

Give Me the Noise

At inconvenient intervals throughout the night,
Desperately wailing to be held close and tight.
When you're at your wits end, what will make it alright?

Give me the noise.

Tiresome interruptions and incessant questions,
when you're already empty from sleep deprivation.
Listening to a humdrum of good natured suggestions...

Give me the noise.

Crying because you flushed the toilet, not him,
or because he was informed that in the bath you can't swim,
or his little sister's arm accidentally brushed his limb...

Give me the noise.

That red-faced strain and squelchy slurp,
a splattered floor from a projectile burp,
a bug she had caught from that snot-faced twerp...

Give me the noise.

The nonsensical words and songs on repeat,
loudly clapping his hands and stamping his feet.
The need to divulge his bowel habits to those on the
street,
including the lady with a smile so sweet,
who dreams of a baby that she'll never meet
but can imagine hearing his soft heartbeat...
she says...
Give me the noise.

I'd Rather have

A sticky hand print on the window pane.
A questionably pink raspberry stain.
Puzzle pieces stashed under the chair.
A dinosaur placed on every stair.

Blobs of Weetabix solidifying on the floor.
Lego bricks in your knicker drawer.
A bath tub full of plastic boats.
Cars in the pockets of everyone's coats.
An entire cupboard of tiny plates and bowls.
A laundry load of clothes for dolls.

A gallery of random squiggles
A house full of high-pitched giggles.
A constant routine of tidying up.
Sipping tea from a stone-cold cup.
Saggy boobs and a wobbly tum
The price I pay for being Mum.

But I wouldn't change it, not a bit,
even if my house looks like shit,
or if my dreams have been put on hold,
or I'm always waking feeling freezing cold
because the kids have stolen the sheets

(even though I said I'd never co-sleep).

Now my priorities have totally changed
after my internal organs have been rearranged
by growing a person within my skin,
accessorising my outfits with a coloured muslin,
then that's what I'd rather have.

It's Not You

I really appreciate your offer
to babysit my brood
but I'm afraid this time
I'll politely decline.
I hope I don't seem rude.

You see we're all still new to this
We're trying to find our feet.
I want them near
in these first few years.
They just make me feel complete.

Plus I know that I would panic
if you took them off my hands.
They wouldn't die,
they would survive
and I know you'd treat them grand,

But I need to be in full control,
just in case the worst should happen.
I must be there
in charge of care.
I know this feeling's common.

For I'm their only mummy
and I know them best, it's true.
I calm them down
when they start to frown.
Sometimes only Mum will do.

One day I'll probably jump up
and accept your offer gladly.
But, now, please understand
why I decline your hand;
It isn't you, it's me.

World Records

If you look in the book or trawl the internet,
you won't find a record for parenting, yet.
No 'World's Cleanest House' or 'Most Laundry Done'
or 'Who took their steps well before they were One',

No 'Earliest First Word' or 'Most Matching Socks'
or 'Most Imaginative Thing You Can Do With a Box'
No records exist for who slept through first,
or for having so many toys that the room's fit to burst.

No trophies dispatched for the most original name,
or the longest version of the peekaboo game.
No shout outs to those who made each meal from
scratch,
Or those who enjoy food from their own vegetable
patch.

No honours were presented for the cutest dribble bib
or for successfully getting the baby to sleep in his crib.
No certificates were produced for just using Entonox,
or the world's sexiest mum wearing post-caesarean
socks.
No awards have been given for snapping back quick,

or looking half decent without some filtering trick.

No gifts were offered to those who always said 'Yes',
Or to those who pushed on when they didn't feel their
best.
No, you won't get a World Record so just do want you
can,
Don't make comparisons between your life and
Instagram.
And if someone makes a comment that's malicious or
mean
tell them to stick it where it can't be seen.

Like what you've read?

Follow me:

@poet_postpartum (Twitter)

@postpartumpoet (Instgram)

@postpartumpoetry (Facebook)

www.postpartumpoetry.co.uk

Printed in Great Britain
by Amazon

35937406R00033